CW00972571

The Art of Good Food

STUFFED VEGETABLES

The Art of Good Food

STUFFED VEGETABLES

JON HIGGINS

Illustrated by

PAUL COLLICUT

TIGER BOOKS INTERNATIONAL
LONDON

The Art of Good Food

STUFFED VEGETABLES

Designed and created by

THE BRIDGEWATER BOOK COMPANY LTD

Designer Sarah Stanley

Editor Donna Wood

Managing Editor Anna Clarkson

Illustrations Paul Collicut

Page make-up Heidi Green

CLB 4591

This edition published 1996 by

Tiger Books International PLC, Twickenham

© 1995 CLB PUBLISHING

Godalming, Surrey

All rights reserved.

Origination by Sussex Repro Ltd England

Printed and bound in Singapore by Tien Wah Press

ISBN 1-85501-774-1

Contents

Introduction

Most of us can remember sitting at the dinner table feeling sorry for ourselves and being told: 'Eat up all your vegetables, they're good for you' which would later progress to: 'If you don't eat them, you won't get any pudding'.

Confronted by a plate of uninspiring and often overcooked vegetables that never strayed beyond the safe realm of the more-common varieties, is it any wonder that many of us turned away from what was potentially the most exciting and healthiest part of the meal, and have probably carried a mental note to eat only the minimum of vegetables ever since?

However, in recent years there has been increasing evidence that properly cooked vegetables, besides containing lots of essential vitamins, have the ability to help our bodies fight off illness and disease.

Knowing we should increase our vegetable intake is all well and good, but a dim recollection of soggy Brussels sprouts and anaemic carrots still deters many people from taking this course. This collection of recipes is designed to rekindle interest in not only the common varieties of vegetable but also some more unusual types that are not often featured in recipe books. From the humble jacket potato to the globe artichoke and custard squash there are recipes to cater for many different occasions and to suit a wide variety of tastes.

USEFUL TIPS ON BUYING VEGETABLES

1. If you buy your vegetables from a supermarket or a similar self-service style shop don't always pick those at the top of the pile. If the retailer correctly rotates his stock this will correspondingly be the oldest, and while there may be nothing wrong with it on the day of purchase, it will be the first to deteriorate later, an important factor to consider if you do not plan to use the item for a couple of days.

2. A perfect-looking vegetable is not always the one with the most flavour. Be discerning, try several different varieties and decide which you prefer, regardless of which is the most visually perfect.

3. In most supermarkets fruit and vegetables are the first goods to be placed into the trolley, and often end up squashed. Try to keep an area in your shopping trolley solely for these delicate items.

4. When buying certain vegetables, such as broccoli, by loose weight, remember that you are paying for a length of useless stalk that will just be thrown away!

5. Once you get your vegetables home, remove any cellophane wrappings. If this is not done condensation will form and the vegetables will deteriorate rapidly.

6. Vegetables last longer stored in a cool, dry place with plenty of ventilation, but of course the sooner you use them the fresher they taste.

7. Any trimmings from fresh vegetables or vegetables slightly past their peak are ideal for making fresh stock. Place them in a saucepan, cover with water and simmer gently for about 30 minutes. If you have no immediate use for the stock, allow it to cool completely before pouring into suitable containers and placing in the freezer.

Home - made Mayonnaise

S*everal recipes in this book use mayonnaise, and as fresh mayonnaise is so much more delicious than shop-bought varieties, I have included a recipe that is simplicity itself.*

INGREDIENTS

2 egg yolks

15ml/1tbsp lemon juice

300ml/10fl oz olive oil

5ml/1tsp English mustard powder

1.75ml/^{1}/$_4$ tsp salt

1.75ml/^{1}/$_4$ tsp freshly ground black pepper

15ml/1tbsp white wine vinegar

▌ Place the egg yolks, lemon juice, salt and mustard powder in a bowl and beat thoroughly for a couple of minutes until all the ingredients are blended together.

▌ Slowly add the olive oil a little at a time, beating well between each addition, until the sauce becomes thick and smooth. This process takes a little time to complete so do not be tempted to rush by adding the oil too quickly as this may cause the mayonnaise to separate.

▌ If separation does occur, place a fresh egg yolk in a mixing bowl and gradually beat the mayonnaise into it. This will correct the consistency.

▌ To finish the mayonnaise stir in the pepper and wine vinegar and chill in the refrigerator until required.

Cabbage Leaves with Chicken & Nut Stuffing

SERVES 6

This hearty recipe will satisfy the most ravenous of appetites

INGREDIENTS

1 large savoy cabbage

225g/8oz cooked chicken, finely chopped

125g/4oz long grain rice, cooked

125g/4oz chopped walnuts

1 egg, beaten

salt and freshly ground black pepper

50g/2oz Parmesan cheese, grated

FOR THE SAUCE

1 medium onion, chopped

30ml/2tbsp olive oil

400g/14oz can chopped tomatoes

15ml/1tbsp tomato purée

50ml/2fl oz clear honey

❚ Using a sharp knife cut the leaves off the cabbage at the stalk and carefully remove them one at a time. Discard the outermost leaves and rinse the remainder under cold water.

❚ Bring a large saucepan of water to the boil and drop in three or four leaves at a time. Push them under the surface with a slotted spoon and leave until soft and pliable. Remove from the water and allow to drain. Repeat this process until all the leaves are blanched.

❚ Mix together the cooked chicken, rice and chopped walnuts and bind them together with the beaten egg. Season the mixture with plenty of salt and black pepper.

❚ Cut away the very hard stalk at the base of each cabbage leaf and place a tablespoon of stuffing in the centre. Roll the cabbage leaf tightly, folding in the sides to create a neat parcel.

❚ Place the stuffed leaves seam-side down in a lightly greased ovenproof dish. Pack the leaves tightly until the dish is full.

❚ To make the sauce, fry the chopped onion in the olive oil until softened and lightly browned. Add the canned tomatoes and tomato purée to the pan and bring to the boil for a few minutes to reduce slightly.

❚ Stir in the honey and season well.

❚ Pour the sauce evenly over the stuffed cabbage and place the dish in a preheated oven at 190°C/375°F/Gas Mark 5 for approximately 45 minutes.

❚ 10 minutes before cooking is complete, sprinkle the Parmesan cheese over the top of the cabbage and return the dish to the oven. The cheese will melt and form a delicious crust. Serve immediately.

TIME: *Preparation takes about 45 minutes.*
Cooking takes approximately 1 hour 15 minutes.

12

Potato & Bacon-stuffed Vine Leaves

SERVES 4

These potato parcels taste great in tomato sauce

INGREDIENTS

1 packet vine leaves in brine (approx. 16 leaves)

450g/16oz new potatoes

salt and freshly ground black pepper

50g/2oz butter

2 cloves garlic, roughly chopped

225g/8oz unsmoked streaky bacon, rind removed

30ml/2tbsp chopped parsley

FOR THE SAUCE

30ml/2tbsp olive oil

1 medium onion, finely chopped

2 cloves garlic, finely chopped

400g/14oz can chopped tomatoes

15ml/1tbsp tomato purée

15ml/1tbsp sugar

Remove the vine leaves from their packaging, place them in a shallow bowl and cover with cold water. Set aside for 20 minutes then drain off the water and carefully separate the leaves. Lay them out on absorbent kitchen paper to absorb the excess moisture.

Scrub any excess soil from the potatoes and boil them in plenty of salted water until they are slightly undercooked, drain and allow to cool.

Melt the butter in a frying pan over a low heat. Turn up the heat and fry the garlic until golden brown.

Cut the bacon into 1cm/½in pieces, add to the pan and fry until crispy and brown.

While the bacon is frying cut the potatoes into slices, add to the pan and toss them regularly until they brown also. Do not worry if the potatoes break up a little.

Remove the frying pan from the heat and add the chopped parsley and plenty of black pepper.

To make the sauce, heat the olive oil in a saucepan and fry the onion and garlic until soft. Add the chopped tomatoes and tomato purée and bring the sauce to the boil. Allow a few minutes for the sauce to reduce. Stir in the sugar, add some seasoning and remove from the heat.

Spoon a small amount of the potato mixture into the centre of a vine leaf and roll it up, folding in the sides to produce a neat, square parcel. Repeat the process with the other vine leaves and arrange them in a lightly greased ovenproof dish.

If there is any potato mixture left, spread it over the stuffed vine leaves and pour the tomato sauce over, ensuring it gets between them.

Cover tightly with foil and place in a preheated oven at 190°C/375°F/Gas Mark 5 for 45 minutes. Serve immediately.

TIME: *Preparation takes about 30 minutes. Cooking takes approximately 1 hour 15 minutes.*

14

*M*oussaka

SERVES 4

A *new way to serve this well-known and much-loved dish*

INGREDIENTS
2 medium aubergines

salt

olive oil

1 large onion, finely chopped

2 cloves garlic, finely chopped

450g/16oz minced lamb

30ml/2tbsp tomato purée

400g/14oz can chopped tomatoes

FOR THE SAUCE
37g/1^1/$_2$oz butter

37g/1^1/$_2$oz flour

600ml/20fl oz fresh milk

50g/2oz grated Parmesan cheese

salt and freshly ground black pepper

Cut the aubergines in half lengthways and carefully remove some of the centre from each half using a teaspoon. Discard. Put the aubergine halves in a colander, sprinkle liberally with salt and leave for 30 minutes. This will extract the bitter juices.

Rinse the aubergines under cold running water, pat dry using absorbent kitchen paper and set to one side.

Heat 30ml/2tbsp of olive oil in a saucepan and fry the onion and garlic until softened and browned a little.

Add the minced lamb to the pan and continue frying until it too has browned, add the tomato purée and stir into the lamb mixture.

Pour in chopped tomatoes and season with plenty of salt and pepper. Leave on a low heat for approximately 30 minutes to allow the meat to fully cook and the flavours to infuse.

While the meat is simmering prepare the white sauce. Melt the butter over a gentle heat and stir in the flour. Allow the flour a minute or two to cook, stirring constantly. Add the milk slowly and a little at a time, stirring until it has all been incorporated. Set to one side.

Heat 30ml/2tbsp olive oil in a frying pan and fry the aubergine halves until they begin to soften and brown a little. Remove from the pan and arrange them in a deep ovenproof dish.

Fill the aubergines with the meat sauce and pour the white sauce over the top of the meat and between the aubergines. Finish by sprinkling the grated Parmesan over the top and grinding over lots of black pepper.

Place in a preheated oven at 180°C/350°F/Gas Mark 4 for 25–30 minutes until the cheese has melted and the surface is a lovely golden brown.

TIME: *Preparation takes about 20 minutes, plus standing.*

Cooking takes approximately 1 hour 20 minutes.

Roasted Chilli Marrow

SERVES 4

A*n inexpensive dish that's tasty and filling*

INGREDIENTS

90ml/6tbsp olive oil

1 small onion, chopped

225g/8oz lean minced beef

15ml/1tbsp medium chilli sauce

400g/14oz can chopped tomatoes

125g/4oz can red kidney beans, drained

1 marrow

salt and freshly ground black pepper

flour for coating

❚ Heat 30ml/2tbsp of the olive oil in a saucepan and fry the chopped onion until softened.

❚ Add the minced beef to the pan and continue frying until the meat has sealed and browned lightly. Stir in the chilli sauce, chopped tomatoes and kidney beans and bring to the boil.

❚ Season generously and reduce the heat. Allow the sauce to simmer gently for approximately 30 minutes so that all the flavours infuse and the meat becomes tender.

❚ Peel the marrow and cut it in half lengthways. Using a spoon, remove all the seeds and discard.

❚ Using a slotted spoon fill the 2 cavities in the marrow halves with the cooked mince, allowing most of the sauce to drain back into the saucepan.

❚ Tie the 2 stuffed halves of marrow back together with string in a couple of places and generously sieve flour over it to coat.

❚ Preheat the oven to 180°C/350°F/Gas Mark 4 and place the remaining olive oil in a roasting pan in the oven to heat through.

❚ When sufficiently hot, place the marrow in the pan and cook until the flesh is tender. Spoon over the juices regularly and season a couple of times during roasting.

❚ When cooked, carefully remove the marrow from the pan and holding it together snip the string. Open up the marrow and place it on a serving dish.

❚ Reheat the sauce that the meat was cooked in and spoon it over the marrow halves. Serve immediately.

TIME: *Preparation takes about 25 minutes. Cooking takes approximately 1 hour.*

16

Roasted Peppers with Bacon & Pasta

SERVES 4

The combination of pepper and pasta is very Italian

INGREDIENTS

2 large red peppers

2 large yellow peppers

olive oil

175g/6oz farfalle

6 rashers smoked streaky bacon

15ml/1tbsp green pesto

15ml/1tbsp fresh basil, chopped

30ml/2tbsp Parmesan cheese, grated

salt and freshly ground black pepper

❚ Cut the peppers in half lengthways and deseed. Brush with a little olive oil and lay on a baking sheet.

❚ Place in a preheated oven at 190°C/375°F/Gas Mark 5 until the peppers soften and the skins begin to blister and char. This will take approximately 15 minutes.

❚ While the peppers are cooking, bring a large saucepan of salted water to the boil. Add a few drops of oil to the pan to prevent sticking and throw in the pasta. Cook the pasta until just tender *(al dente)*.

❚ Place the bacon rashers on a wire rack under a preheated grill and cook until very dry and crispy. Remove and crumble them between the fingers.

❚ Drain the cooked pasta thoroughly and tip it into a bowl, stir in the bacon, pesto, Parmesan, chopped basil and lots of pepper.

❚ The peppers should now be roasted to perfection. Remove them from the oven and carefully transfer them to their serving dishes.

❚ Pile spoonfuls of the pasta mixture into each pepper half and drizzle over a little extra olive oil.

❚ Serve immediately with lots of crusty bread to mop up the excess oil.

TIME: *Preparation takes about 10 minutes. Cooking takes approximately 20 minutes.*

Stuffed Cucumber in White Wine Sauce

SERVES 4

You can use cucumber for so much more than just salads

INGREDIENTS

1 large or 2 medium cucumbers

30ml/2tbsp olive oil

1 medium onion, finely chopped

175g/6oz mushrooms, finely chopped

125g/4oz thin sliced ham, finely chopped

5ml/1tsp dried coriander

75ml/3fl oz white wine

150ml/5fl oz single cream

15ml/1tbsp fresh parsley, chopped

olive oil

salt and freshly ground black pepper

Wipe the cucumber, remove the ends and cut into 4 equal lengths. Cut each piece in half and remove the seeds using a teaspoon. Set to one side.

To prepare the stuffing, heat the olive oil in a frying pan and fry the onion until soft, do not allow it to colour. Add the chopped mushrooms to the pan and stir into the onion; continue frying until the mushrooms have absorbed some of the pan juices and become darker in colour.

Add the ham and dried coriander to the pan and stir into the stuffing with plenty of seasoning.

Arrange the prepared cucumber in a lightly greased ovenproof dish and place spoonfuls of the stuffing into the hollowed out centres. Spread any remaining stuffing over the top.

Drizzle over a little olive oil and lightly season with salt and pepper.

Place in a preheated oven at 180°C/350°F/Gas Mark 4 for approximately 20 minutes or until the cucumber is tender.

Just before the cooking time is complete, reheat the frying pan for a few seconds and pour in the wine. This will lift any of the stuffing still left in the pan and add flavour to the sauce.

Reduce the wine briefly and remove the pan from the heat. Stir in the cream and add the chopped parsley and a little seasoning.

Arrange the stuffed cucumber in a serving dish and spoon a little of the sauce over each piece. Serve immediately.

TIME: *Preparation takes about 20 minutes. Cooking takes approximately 45 minutes.*

19

Aubergine with Kabanos

SERVES 4

This Polish pork sausage is now widely available

INGREDIENTS

2 medium aubergines

salt and freshly ground black pepper

2 cloves garlic, thinly sliced

2 medium onions, thinly sliced

8 Kabanos sausages

225g/8oz large flat mushrooms, thinly sliced

30ml/2tbsp parsley, finely chopped

60ml/4tbsp fresh breadcrumbs

60ml/4tbsp olive oil

Cut the aubergines in half lengthways and sprinkle with salt. Leave them for approximately 30 minutes to extract the juices, then wash off the salt and pat dry with absorbent kitchen paper.

Make deep cuts into the flesh of the aubergine halves and place them in an ovenproof dish, sprinkle generously with water and cover tightly with foil.

Place in a preheated oven at 180°C/350°F/Gas Mark 4 for approximately 45 minutes or until the flesh has softened. Keep a watchful eye on them as you do not want them to overcook and lose their shape.

While they are cooking prepare the filling. Fry the onion and garlic in 30ml/2tbsp of olive oil until they are golden brown. Spoon them onto absorbent kitchen paper and set aside.

Remove the skin from the kabanos and cut them into 1cm/^{1}/$_2$-inch chunks. Heat the remaining olive oil and fry briefly until lightly browned.

Add the mushrooms to the pan. Toss them among the sausages so they absorb the olive oil and cooking juices. Return the cooked onion and garlic to the pan and briefly fry the whole lot together. Season generously with plenty of salt and pepper.

When the aubergines are cooked, scoop out the flesh leaving a good 1cm/^{1}/$_2$-inch thickness next to the skin. Chop half of the removed flesh and stir it into the filling.

Pile the filling into the aubergine shells and arrange them on a baking sheet.

Mix together the chopped parsley, breadcrumbs and a few twists of black pepper and sprinkle the mixture generously over the stuffed aubergines. Drizzle a small amount of olive oil over the top of each one.

Place them in the oven for 20 minutes to heat through thoroughly and serve immediately.

TIME: *Preparation takes about 25 minutes, plus standing.*
Cooking takes approximately 1 hour.

21

Stuffed Custard Squash

SERVES 4

Custard squashes are available during summer and should be used when very ripe

INGREDIENTS

1 ripe custard squash

1 large onion, chopped

2 cloves garlic, chopped

30ml/2tbsp olive oil

350g/12oz lean minced beef

15ml/1tbsp tomato purée

400g/14oz can chopped tomatoes

400g/14oz can red kidney beans, drained

salt and freshly ground black pepper

45ml/3tbsp Red Leicester cheese, grated

‖ Cut the top from the squash and remove all the seeds using a spoon. Set to one side. Preheat the oven to 190°C/375°F/Gas Mark 5.

‖ Heat the olive oil in a saucepan and cook the onion and garlic until soft and nicely browned. Add the minced beef to the pan and cook until sealed and just beginning to brown.

‖ Stir in the tomato purée, chopped tomatoes and kidney beans and season generously with salt and black pepper. Bring the pan to the boil, then reduce the heat and allow to simmer, stirring occasionally, for approximately 30 minutes until the meat is tender. If the sauce begins to look a little dry at any stage during cooking add a little cold water.

‖ When the meat sauce is cooked, spoon it into the squash and sprinkle over the grated cheese.

‖ Place the stuffed squash on a baking tray and place in the oven for 30 minutes. Keep an eye on it while it is cooking as it is a thin-skinned vegetable with tender flesh, so you may find the cooking time can be reduced depending on its ripeness.

‖ Place the cooked squash on a large serving platter. Serve with plenty of salt and pepper and some extra cheese for sprinkling.

TIME: *Preparation takes about 20 minutes. Cooking takes approximately 1 hour 10 minutes.*

Stuffed Courgettes in Cheese Sauce

SERVES 4

The humble courgette has never tasted this good

INGREDIENTS
4 large courgettes
30ml/2tbsp olive oil
1 small onion, finely chopped
2 cloves garlic, crushed
1 carrot, roughly chopped
125g/4oz rindless bacon, chopped
225g/8oz fresh minced beef
30ml/2tbsp tomato purée
150ml/5fl oz red wine
150ml/5fl oz beef stock
salt and freshly ground black pepper

FOR THE CHEESE SAUCE
12g/¹/₂oz butter
12g/¹/₂oz flour
300ml/10fl oz fresh milk
125g/4oz Cheddar cheese, grated

Bring a large saucepan of water to the boil and drop in the courgettes to blanch for 10 minutes.

Remove the blanched courgettes from the water and cut them in half lengthways. Use a teaspoon to remove some of the flesh from the centres. Arrange them in a lightly greased ovenproof dish. Set aside.

Heat the olive oil in a saucepan and fry the onion and garlic until softened and lightly browned. Add the carrot and bacon and continue frying until the bacon is cooked.

Add the minced beef to the pan and fry briefly until the meat is sealed. Stir in the tomato purée and continue frying for a couple of minutes.

Pour in the wine and beef stock and season well. Reduce the heat, and simmer for 30 minutes, stirring occasionally, until tender and reduced in quantity.

Melt the butter in a saucepan and stir in the flour. Cook briefly for a minute or two then slowly stir in the milk until you have a smooth sauce. Add half the grated cheese to the sauce and season well.

Spoon the meat into the hollowed-out courgettes and pour any remaining over the top. Cover with the cheese sauce and sprinkle the remaining grated cheese over the top.

Finish with a few twists of fresh pepper and place in a preheated oven at 180°C/350°F/Gas Mark 4 for 30 minutes until the dish is well heated through and the cheese has melted to a lovely crust.

Serve immediately accompanied by a crisp green salad.

TIME: *Preparation takes about 20 minutes. Cooking takes approximately 1 hour 30 minutes.*

24

Stuffed Fennel

SERVES 4

This is a great way to enjoy the unique flavour of fennel

INGREDIENTS

4 large fennel bulbs

30ml/2tbsp olive oil

1 small onion, finely chopped

2 cloves garlic, finely chopped

225g/8oz lean minced beef

15ml/1tbsp tomato purée

15ml/1tbsp medium hot chilli sauce

fresh breadcrumbs

salt and freshly ground black pepper

Cut the stalks from the top of the fennel and place the bulbs in a steamer. Steam for about 30 minutes or until they begin to soften. Do not overcook or they will fall apart.

While the fennel is cooking prepare the meat stuffing. Heat the olive oil in a frying pan and fry the onion and garlic until they have softened and browned a little.

Add the minced beef to the pan and fry it until it is sealed and beginning to brown. Add the tomato purée and chilli sauce along with sufficient cold water to moisten.

Season the sauce well and allow to simmer for about 30 minutes, adding a little more water as and when necessary to prevent it from drying out.

When the fennel has finished steaming, carefully ease open the outer leaves, and using a sharp knife, make cuts into the inside of the fennel. Using a teaspoon, scoop out the insides leaving a good thickness of 'shell'.

Roughly chop the fennel insides and stir them into the meat sauce.

Arrange the fennel bulbs in a lightly greased ovenproof dish and spoon the meat sauce into them. Spoon any remaining sauce over the top of the bulbs, and sprinkle thickly with breadcrumbs.

Season the finished dish with plenty of black pepper and place in a preheated oven at 180°C/350°F/Gas Mark 4 for 15–20 minutes until well heated through. Serve immediately.

TIME: *Preparation takes about 20 minutes. Cooking takes approximately 1 hour.*

Whole Stuffed Cabbage

SERVES 6

Amaze your fellow diners with this impressive-looking dish

INGREDIENTS
1 savoy cabbage
1 small onion, finely chopped
450g/1lb best quality sausagemeat
15ml/1tbsp tomato purée
salt and freshly ground black pepper

Discard any rough-looking or loose leaves from the cabbage so you are left with the tightly packed heart.

With a sharp knife cut the top from the cabbage and carefully remove the insides leaving a 'wall' about 2.5cm/1inch thick all the way around.

Bring a large saucepan of water to the boil and blanch the cabbage shell and top for 5 minutes until it just begins to soften. Remove and drain thoroughly.

Using your hands, mix together the chopped onion, sausagemeat and tomato purée and season well. Stuff the inside of the cabbage with the sausagemeat mix and use a few leaves from the top of the cabbage to cover.

Tie the cabbage tightly in a double thickness of muslin and place in a saucepan of boiling water for an hour.

When cooked, carefully remove the cabbage from the saucepan and drain thoroughly. Remove the muslin and place the whole cabbage on a serving dish. Cut the stuffed cabbage into 6 portions at the table.

TIME: *Preparation takes about 20 minutes. Cooking takes approximately 1 hour.*

Radishes with Pâté

MAKES APPROXIMATELY 30

These make great little 'pop-in-the-mouth' appetisers to serve before a meal

INGREDIENTS
1 bunch of large radishes
125g/4oz pâté de foie gras (or similar)
50g/2oz butter
salt and freshly ground black pepper
poppy seeds (for decoration)

This recipe successfully combines the radish, much used as an hors-d'oeuvre in Lebanese cookery, with the very French pâté de foie gras.

Cut the stalks and roots from the radishes to provide a flat surface to stand on. Wash the trimmed radishes under cold running water and cut them in half widthways.

Using a melon baller, remove a portion of the white centre of the radish and discard. Keep the prepared radishes in a bowl of cold water until you fill them.

In a separate bowl, pound together the butter and pâté with a little seasoning until they are well mixed and nicely softened. Spoon the mixture into a small piping bag with a decorative nozzle.

Drain the radish halves and dry on absorbent kitchen paper, then pipe in a rosette of the pâté mixture so that it stands just proud of the top of the radish.

When all the radish halves are stuffed, stand them close together on their serving dish and sprinkle liberally with poppy seeds. Keep refrigerated before serving.

TIME: *Preparation takes about 20 minutes.*

26

Lebanese-style Courgettes

SERVES 4

These stuffed courgettes are a meal in themselves

INGREDIENTS
30ml/2tbsp olive oil
1 small onion, finely chopped
2 cloves garlic, crushed
125g/4oz brown rice, washed
50g/2oz pine nuts
350g/12oz minced lamb
pinch of cinnamon, ground cloves and ground chilli
freshly ground black pepper
6 medium courgettes
300ml/10fl oz red wine
300ml/10fl oz beef stock
cornflour to thicken the sauce

Heat the olive oil and gently fry the onion and garlic until soft. Stir in the washed rice and pine nuts and fry briefly to coat them with oil.

Remove the pan from the heat and spoon the mixture into a food processor. Briefly process until the mixture is coarsely chopped.

Pound the minced lamb and spices in a pestle and mortar until smooth then place in a mixing bowl along with the rice mixture.

Using your hands, mix the two together thoroughly and season with plenty of black pepper.

Slice the ends from the courgettes and carefully remove as much of the flesh as possible, leaving a thin layer next to the skin, using an apple corer.

Pack each courgette as full as possible with the stuffing mix and place them side-by-side in a shallow, lightly greased ovenproof dish.

Pour over the red wine and beef stock, cover and place in a preheated oven at 190°C/375°F/Gas Mark 5 for approximately 30 minutes or until the courgettes are tender.

When cooked, remove the stuffed courgettes from the oven, arrange on a serving dish and keep hot.

Thicken the cooking liquor with a little cornflour dissolved in water and spoon over the courgettes. Serve immediately.

TIME: *Preparation takes about 30 minutes. Cooking takes approximately 30 minutes.*

Couscous Red Cabbage

Serves 4

Red cabbage and couscous make an excellent partnership

INGREDIENTS

1 red cabbage

225g/8oz couscous

175g/6oz cooked lamb, shredded

125g/4oz dried apricots, finely chopped

600ml/20fl oz vegetable stock

salt and freshly ground black pepper

Remove the rough outer leaves from the cabbage until you are left with the tightly packed heart. Carefully remove the leaves one at a time taking care not to damage them.

Bring a large saucepan of water to the boil and drop in the cabbage leaves for a few minutes to sufficiently soften them so they can be rolled. Blanch a few at a time so you do not overcook them.

Remove the leaves from the water and lay them on absorbent kitchen paper to soak up any excess moisture. Use a sharp knife to cut away the hard stalk at the base of the leaves.

Spread out the couscous in a heatproof dish and cover with boiling water. Set to one side for 15–20 minutes until the couscous has absorbed the water and is ready to use.

Stir the lamb and dried apricots into the couscous and season well.

Spoon some couscous stuffing mixture onto the middle of the cabbage leaves and roll them up, folding the sides in as you roll. Place the stuffed leaves seam-side down in a lightly greased ovenproof dish.

When the dish is full, pour over sufficient stock to cover the base of the dish and cover with foil. Bake in a preheated oven at 180°C/350°F/Gas Mark 4 for 30 minutes or until the cabbage leaves are tender.

Carefully remove the stuffed leaves from the stock with a slotted spoon and arrange them on a serving dish.

TIME: *Preparation takes about 25 minutes. Cooking takes approximately 1 hour.*

Stuffed Vine Leaves

SERVES 4

These are a great favourite of the Russians but are equally popular here

INGREDIENTS

1 packet vine leaves in brine (approx. 16 leaves)

15ml/1tbsp olive oil

2 shallots, finely chopped

175g/6oz minced lamb

5ml/1tsp hot chilli sauce

50g/2oz wild rice, cooked

25g/1oz sultanas

25g/1oz pine nuts

30ml/2tbsp chopped fresh mint

salt and freshly ground black pepper

300ml/10fl oz chicken stock

Greek yoghurt, to serve (optional)

30

▌Remove the vine leaves from their packaging, place in a shallow bowl and cover with cold water. Set aside for 20 minutes then drain off the water and carefully separate the leaves. Lay them out on absorbent kitchen paper to absorb the excess moisture.

▌Heat the olive oil in a frying pan and briefly fry the chopped shallots until softened. Add the minced lamb and continue to cook until the meat is sealed and just beginning to brown. Add the chilli sauce.

▌Stir in the wild rice, sultanas, pine nuts and chopped fresh mint and season well.

▌Place a tablespoon of the lamb mixture in the centre of a vine leaf, fold in the sides and roll up to form a neat, tight parcel.

▌Repeat this process with the remaining vine leaves and pack them into the bottom of a saucepan. If the saucepan is not big enough cover the first layer with a couple of spare vine leaves and begin a second.

▌When all the vine leaves are stuffed, pour over the chicken stock, cover with a lid and place over a low heat to simmer for approximately 45 minutes.

▌When cooked, carefully remove the stuffed leaves from the stock with a slotted spoon and arrange on a serving dish. Alternatively, leave to cool and serve with Greek yoghurt flavoured with a little chopped mint.

TIME: *Preparation takes about 30 minutes. Cooking takes approximately 50 minutes.*

Radicchio Leaves with Coconut Chicken

MAKES 12

The bitter radicchio leaves taste wonderful with the sweet chicken

INGREDIENTS

1 whole fresh coconut

2 ripe bananas

juice of 2 limes

350g/12oz cooked chicken breast

25ml/1fl oz olive oil

12 radicchio leaves

25g/1oz flaked almonds, toasted

Drill two small holes at one end of the coconut and drain off the milk, then give the shell a sharp tap with a hammer to get to the flesh.

Peel and chop the bananas into 20mm/^{3}/$_4$-inch chunks, and roll them in a little of the lime juice to prevent them from discolouring.

Cut the chicken into similar sized pieces and mix these with the banana chunks.

Put the remaining lime juice, olive oil, 25ml/1fl oz coconut milk and 15ml/1tbsp grated coconut in a screw-top jar with a tight-fitting lid and shake thoroughly to mix.

Pour the marinade over the chicken and banana and stir. Cover and leave to marinate for at least an hour.

When the chicken has marinated, carefully remove it from the liquid using a slotted spoon and divide it equally between the radicchio leaves.

Sprinkle a few lightly toasted almond flakes over the top of each leaf and roll them up, secure each roll with a cocktail stick and arrange on a serving dish. Keep refrigerated before serving.

TIME: *Preparation takes about 25 minutes, plus marinating.*

31

Wild Rice Boats

SERVES 4

*T*hese not only taste great, but look attractive when served

INGREDIENTS

2 medium aubergines

salt and freshly ground black pepper

175g/6oz wild rice, washed

chicken stock

8 rashers unsmoked streaky bacon

olive oil

50g/2oz black olives, pitted and sliced

50g/2oz frozen peas, defrosted

butter

Cut the aubergines in half lengthways, sprinkle the cut surface with plenty of salt and leave to stand for 30 minutes. Wash off the salt and extracted juices and dry with absorbent kitchen paper.

Score the flesh with a sharp knife, but do not pierce the skin. Place the aubergines in an ovenproof dish with a sprinkling of water. Cover and cook in a moderate oven at 180°C/350°F/Gas Mark 4 until the flesh is soft. Take care not to overcook the aubergines in case they collapse.

While they are cooking, put the rice in a saucepan with sufficient chicken stock to just cover it. Do not add any salt as the stock will be sufficiently salty. Place the pan on the heat and bring to the boil, reduce to a simmer and cook the rice until most of the stock has been absorbed and the grains are still slightly firm. Strain to remove any excess liquid and set to one side.

Chop the bacon into 1cm/^{1}/$_2$-inch lengths and fry it in a little olive oil until nicely browned and crispy.

Put the cooked rice, bacon, sliced olives and peas in a mixing bowl and stir together with plenty of black pepper.

Scoop out the aubergine flesh leaving a thin layer next to the skin, roughly chop and add to the rice mixture.

Generously fill the skins with the rice mixture and put a small knob of butter on top of each.

Place the stuffed aubergine skins on a baking sheet and return them to the oven for 15–20 minutes until heated through. Serve immediately.

TIME: *Preparation takes about 15 minutes, plus standing.*

Cooking takes approximately 45 minutes.

33

ℒazy 𝒥umbo 𝒫rawns

S E R V E S 4

A *recipe to make you yearn for those hot summer days*

I N G R E D I E N T S

18 cooked jumbo prawns, peeled

2 large heads of chicory

frisée and radicchio leaves

1 lemon, sliced

4 cooked jumbo prawns, unpeeled, for decoration

(optional)

F O R T H E M A R I N A D E

50ml/2fl oz virgin olive oil

juice of 1 lemon

salt and freshly ground black pepper

15ml/1tbsp balsamic vinegar

▌Place all the ingredients for the marinade into a screw-top jar and shake well to mix.

▌Place the prawns in a shallow dish and pour the marinade over, gently tossing the prawns to coat them evenly. Cover and refrigerate for a couple of hours.

▌Discard any damaged outer leaves from the chicory and gently break off the inner leaves. Rinse them under cold running water and pat dry with absorbent kitchen paper.

▌Wash sufficient frisée and radicchio lettuce to completely cover a large oval meat platter, drain thoroughly and arrange attractively.

▌Remove the prawns from the marinade and lay one prawn on each piece of chicory. Arrange these on the bed of lettuce.

▌Pour any remaining marinade over the lettuce and garnish with the lemon slices and cooked prawns, if using. Serve with chunks of fresh bread and plenty of chilled white wine.

TIME: *Preparation takes about 25 minutes, plus marinating.*

$\mathscr{A}$vocado $\mathscr{S}$oufflé

SERVES 4

A *lighter way to enjoy avocados*

INGREDIENTS

2 ripe avocados

50g/2oz cooked peeled prawns, mashed

12g/¹⁄₂oz butter

12g/¹⁄₂oz flour

150ml/5fl oz fresh milk

salt and freshly ground black pepper

2 eggs, separated

36

▌Cut the avocados in half lengthways and gently separate the two halves, remove the stone and discard.

▌Using a teaspoon, carefully scoop out all the flesh from the avocados into a bowl taking care not to damage the skins. Mash the avocado flesh to a fine paste and beat together with the mashed prawns, then set to one side with the skins.

▌Over a gentle heat melt the butter in a saucepan, add the flour and stir the two together for a few minutes to allow the flour to cook.

▌Slowly add the milk, a few drops at a time to begin with, then increase the flow until all the milk has been added and the sauce is thick and smooth. Remove the pan from the heat and season with a good pinch of salt and lots of freshly ground black pepper.

▌Beat together the mashed avocado, the sauce and the egg yolks until the mixture is smooth.

▌In a clean bowl whisk the egg whites until they form stiff peaks and fold them into the avocado mixture. Spoon the mixture into the 4 avocado skins and place them on a baking sheet.

▌Bake them in a preheated oven at 200°C/400°F/Gas Mark 6 for approximately 20 minutes or until they are well risen and golden brown. Serve immediately.

TIME: *Preparation takes about 20 minutes. Cooking takes approximately 35 minutes.*

$\mathcal{S}$ardine-stuffed $\mathcal{O}$nions

S E R V E S   4

$\mathcal{O}$nions taste wonderful when roasted in the oven

INGREDIENTS

2 large onions

225g/8oz can sardines in tomato sauce

salt and freshly ground black pepper

50g/2oz long grain rice, cooked

50g/2oz sultanas

fresh breadcrumbs

olive oil

Do not peel the onions. Place them directly onto the shelf of a preheated oven at 200°C/400°F/Gas Mark 6 for 30 minutes.

Remove the sardines from the can and mash them lightly with plenty of seasoning. Stir in the cooked rice and sultanas.

When the onions have had 30 minutes cooking time remove from the oven and peel them. Cut them in half from top to bottom and remove some of the layers from the middle to create an onion bowl.

Fill the hollowed out onions with the sardine stuffing and place them on a baking sheet. Sprinkle generously with the fresh breadcrumbs and drizzle with a little olive oil. Reduce the oven temperature to 180°C/350°F/Gas Mark 6 and return the stuffed onions to cook for a further 20 minutes.

Serve immediately, either as a starter or served with potatoes and vegetables as a main course.

TIME: *Preparation takes about 30 minutes.*
Cooking takes approximately 50 minutes.

Beef Tomato Niçoise

SERVES 4

This is based on a traditional salad recipe but served inside a tomato shell

INGREDIENTS

4 beef tomatoes, evenly sized

50g/2oz pitted black olives, halved

2 hard boiled eggs, roughly chopped

2 red baby bell peppers, seeded and sliced

15ml/1tbsp salted peanuts

handful of rocket leaves, roughly torn

8 anchovy fillets

fresh lettuce leaves, to serve

FOR THE DRESSING

60ml/4 tbsp white wine vinegar

5ml/1tsp Dijon mustard

75ml/3fl oz best quality olive oil

salt and freshly ground black pepper

‖ Wash the beef tomatoes under cold running water and dry using a tea towel.

‖ Slice the tops off the tomatoes and carefully remove the insides using a teaspoon. Discard.

‖ Place the black olives, chopped eggs, sliced peppers, peanuts and rocket in a mixing bowl and gently toss together using your hands.

‖ Place all the ingredients for the dressing in a clean screw-top jar and shake vigorously to combine. Try a little on a teaspoon first to check the taste is to your liking before pouring a small quantity onto the salad and lightly tossing. Do not feel obliged to use all the dressing, it can be refrigerated for future use.

‖ Spoon the dressed salad into the tomato skins, brush the outside of the tomatoes with a little of the dressing to give a shine and finish each tomato with 2 anchovy fillets laid over the top in a cross.

‖ Serve on a bed of fresh lettuce leaves with lots of crusty bread and a twist of black pepper.

TIME: *Preparation takes about 30 minutes.*

Courgettes with Mackerel & Herbs

SERVES 4

This makes a great healthy snack

INGREDIENTS

2 medium courgettes

4 smoked mackerel fillets, cooked and skinned

2 eggs, beaten

30ml/2tbsp olive oil

15ml/1tbsp fresh chopped fennel leaves

15ml/1tbsp fresh tarragon, chopped

50g/2oz red Leicester cheese, grated

salt and freshly ground black pepper

‖ Cut the courgettes in half lengthways and carefully remove the insides using a teaspoon, leaving a thin layer of flesh next to the skin.

‖ Break the smoked mackerel into small pieces and place in a mixing bowl. Moisten the fish with the beaten egg and using a fork, mash the fish to a paste.

‖ Chop the courgette insides and briefly fry them in the olive oil for 5 minutes until they soften. Add to the fish.

‖ Beat the chopped fennel leaves, tarragon and grated cheese into the mackerel mixture and season well.

‖ Spoon the stuffing into the courgette skins and place in a lightly greased ovenproof dish. Cook in a preheated oven at 190°C/375°F/Gas Mark 5 for 20 minutes.

‖ Serve immediately with a small green salad.

TIME: *Preparation takes about 20 minutes. Cooking takes approximately 25 minutes.*

40

Smoked Salmon & Lettuce Rolls

SERVES 4

This is an excellent way of serving smoked salmon without the need for cutlery

INGREDIENTS

1 oak leaf lettuce

12 slices smoked salmon

freshly ground black pepper

lemon juice

lemon wedges, to garnish

‖ Remove the rough outer leaves from the lettuce and carefully pick the 12 choicest leaves from those remaining. Wash in a little cold water and shake to remove the excess moisture. Be gentle with the lettuce leaves during this process as you want them to remain as full of life as possible.

‖ Place a slice of smoked salmon on each leaf, season with plenty of black pepper and sprinkle with a little lemon juice.

‖ Roll the leaf quite tightly in a fan shape and place on a serving dish with the end of the leaf underneath.

‖ Repeat this process with the remaining leaves and pack them tightly together. Garnish with lemon wedges and serve.

TIME: *Preparation takes about 20 minutes.*

Warm Avocado with Creole Prawns

SERVES 4

H*ot avocado tastes great with these fruity prawns*

INGREDIENTS

2 large ripe avocados

1 lime

30ml/2tbsp olive oil

$^1/_2$ bunch spring onions, finely chopped

2 cloves garlic, chopped

2 tomatoes, skinned and chopped

1 red pepper, seeded and chopped

15ml/1tbsp tomato purée

few drops of Tabasco

350g/12oz large cooked peeled prawns

freshly ground black pepper

lime wedges, to garnish

▌ Cut the avocados in half lengthways and gently separate the 2 halves. Remove the stone and discard.

▌ Cut the lime in half and rub it over the cut surface of the avocado. Arrange the avocados in an ovenproof dish and place in a preheated oven at 180°C/350°F/Gas Mark 4 for 10–15 minutes. It is important that the flesh just heats through and does not overcook.

▌ While the avocado is cooking heat the oil in a wok or saucepan and fry the chopped spring onion and garlic for 2 minutes. Add the skinned tomatoes and red pepper and continue frying for a further 2 minutes.

▌ Remove the wok or pan from the heat and stir the tomato purée and a few drops of Tabasco into the vegetables.

▌ Lower the heat. Drain off any liquid from the prawns, return the pan to the heat, fry the prawns briefly for 1 minute.

▌ Squeeze the halves of lime and strain the juice to remove the pips. Add the lime juice to the pan along with a few twists of black pepper.

▌ Remove the warmed avocados from the oven and transfer them to serving dishes. Spoon some of the Creole prawns into the centre of each and serve immediately with lime wedges.

TIME: *Preparation takes about 25 minutes. Cooking takes approximately 15 minutes.*

$\mathcal{A}$ubergine-wrapped $\mathcal{S}$ardines

S E R V E S 4

The cooking juices from the fish are absorbed into the aubergine so no flavour is lost

INGREDIENTS

2 medium aubergines

salt and freshly ground black pepper

8 fresh sardines, trimmed, cleaned and descaled

olive oil

60ml/4tbsp passata or tomato sauce

pitted black olives

tomato or horseradish sauce, to serve

Cut four 1cm/½-inch slices from each aubergine, sprinkle them with salt and allow to stand for 30 minutes to extract the bitter juices.

Rinse off the aubergine slices and pat them dry with absorbent kitchen paper. Set to one side.

Wash the sardines under cold running water and dry thoroughly. Arrange on a foil-covered grill pan, brush with a little olive oil and season well.

Place under a preheated grill and cook briefly for 3 minutes. Turn the fish, brush over some more olive oil and grill again for 3 minutes.

While the sardines are cooking fry each slice of aubergine in 30ml/2tbsp olive oil briefly on each side until it softens and browns a little. Remove from the pan, spread a little passata over the aubergine and place a sardine widthways across the slice.

Carefully fold the aubergine end to end and pin with half a cocktail stick. Stud the end of the cocktail stick with an olive and lay the finished items on a lightly oiled baking sheet.

Place the wrapped sardines in a preheated oven at 180°C/350°F/Gas Mark 4 for 5 minutes then serve immediately, accompanied by a tomato or horseradish sauce.

TIME: *Preparation takes about 30 minutes, plus standing.*

Cooking takes approximately 30 minutes.

45

Mixed Fish Risotto Peppers

SERVES 4

Creamy risotto and seafood in a crisply roasted red pepper

INGREDIENTS

4 large squat red peppers

30ml/2tbsp olive oil

1 small onion, finely chopped

350g/12oz risotto rice

120ml/40fl oz chicken stock

450g/1lb packet, cooked mixed seafood, thawed

salt and freshly ground black pepper

▌ Cut the tops from the peppers and carefully remove the seeds and core. Place the peppers and tops in a large bowl and pour over sufficient boiling water to cover them.

▌ Leave to stand for 5 minutes then pour off the water and leave the peppers upside-down on absorbent kitchen paper to drain thoroughly.

▌ Heat the olive oil in a saucepan and gently fry the chopped onion until soft, but not coloured. Add the rice to the pan and fry for a couple of minutes, tossing with the onion so it becomes thoroughly coated in the oil.

▌ Have the stock simmering close to hand. Pour a ladleful of the hot stock onto the rice and stir until it has been absorbed. Stir the rice constantly while it cooks.

▌ Continue this process of adding the stock a ladleful at a time until the risotto becomes thick and creamy but the rice still has a firmness when bitten. This will take about 20–25 minutes.

▌ When the risotto has finished cooking, drain the thawed seafood and stir it into the rice. Season well.

▌ Place the blanched peppers on a baking sheet and spoon in the risotto until just below the rim of the peppers. Place the lids on top, brush the outsides with a little oil and grind over some black pepper.

▌ Place in a preheated oven at 170°C/325°F/Gas Mark 3 for 35–40 minutes until the pepper is tender. Serve immediately.

TIME: *Preparation takes about 15 minutes. Cooking takes approximately 1 hour 10 minutes.*

Avocado Marie Rose

SERVES 4

A *deservedly popular dish*

INGREDIENTS

2 firm, ripe avocado pears

washed lettuce leaves

1 quantity mayonnaise (see page 11)

15ml/1tbsp tomato purée

dash of Tabasco

freshly ground black pepper

350g/12oz cooked peeled prawns, defrosted if frozen

lemon wedges, to garnish

Cut the avocados in half lengthways, gently ease the 2 halves apart and remove the stone. Line 4 small bowls with a few washed lettuce leaves and put an avocado half in each one.

Put the mayonnaise into a bowl and beat in the tomato purée and Tabasco. Season well.

Gently toss the prawns in the mayonnaise and divide the mixture between the avocados. Do not worry if the mayonnaise runs over the side of the avocado as this adds to the look of the dish.

Garnish with lemon wedges. Serve with thin slices of brown bread and butter and more black pepper.

TIME: *Preparation takes about 15 minutes.*

Chick Pea & Tuna Salad

SERVES 4

T*his delightful salad shows that watching your weight does not have to be boring*

INGREDIENTS

4 iceberg lettuce leaves

1 can chick peas, drained

1 large can tuna chunks in brine

1 bunch salad onions, roughly chopped

25g/1oz raisins

1 quantity mayonnaise (see page 11)

salt and freshly ground black pepper

mint leaves, to garnish (optional)

Place an iceberg lettuce leaf on each serving plate. There is no need to wash them as the leaves are so tightly packed together there is little chance of soil getting between them.

In a mixing bowl combine the salad ingredients and bind the whole lot together with the mayonnaise.

Season well and spoon the salad into the lettuce leaves. Garnish with a few torn mint leaves if desired and serve straightaway.

TIME: *Preparation takes about 15 minutes.*

47

Avocado with Crab & Lime Mayonnaise

SERVES 4

Rich crab meat tastes great mixed with a refreshing home-made mayonnaise

INGREDIENTS

2 firm, ripe avocados

lemon or lime juice

225g/8oz white crab meat

FOR THE MAYONNAISE

2 egg yolks

5ml/1tsp Dijon mustard

300ml/10fl oz olive oil

grated rind of 1 lime

30ml/2tbsp lime juice

pinch of salt and freshly ground black pepper

toasted flaked almonds for decoration

▌Cut the avocados in half lengthways and gently ease the 2 halves apart. Carefully remove the stones. If you are preparing the avocados well in advance of eating, rub the cut surface with a little lemon or lime juice to prevent the flesh from discolouring.

▌Divide the crab meat into 4 and pile it into the avocado halves. Set to one side while you prepare the mayonnaise.

▌Place the egg yolks and Dijon mustard in a mixing bowl and beat vigorously until well blended. Begin beating the olive oil into the mixture very slowly, a few drops at a time. Gradually the mayonnaise will begin to thicken, at this point you can increase the flow of olive oil until it is all incorporated and you have a thick, glossy mayonnaise with a lovely pale yellow colouring.

▌Finish by beating in the grated lime zest juice and season well.

▌Spoon a generous quantity of the mayonnaise over each avocado half and sprinkle a handful of toasted almonds over. Serve with slices of brown bread and butter and the pepper mill.

TIME: *Preparation takes about 25 minutes.*

Red & White Cabbage Parcels in Vinaigrette

SERVES 4

These stuffed leaves can be prepared well in advance

INGREDIENTS

8 red cabbage leaves

8 savoy cabbage leaves

125g/4oz long grain rice, slightly undercooked

25g/1oz sultanas

125g/4oz cooked peeled prawns

15ml/1tbsp tomato purée

salt and freshly ground black pepper

FOR THE VINAIGRETTE

30ml/2tbsp red wine vinegar

60ml/4tbsp olive oil

salt and freshly ground black pepper

Bring a saucepan of water to the boil and blanch the cabbage leaves 1 or 2 at a time until they are pliable enough to roll up but are not overcooked.

Once blanched, remove the leaves from the water and lay them out on absorbent kitchen paper to drain thoroughly.

In a large bowl mix together the cooked rice, sultanas and peeled prawns and bind them all together with the tomato purée. Season well.

Cut away any hard stalk from the base of the cabbage leaves and place a spoonful of the filling in the centre of each one. Roll them up, folding the sides in as you go to form a neat parcel.

Place the parcels in a steamer, seam-side down, and cook for about 30 minutes until the cabbage leaves are tender. Carefully remove them from the steamer and allow to cool completely.

Place all the ingredients for the vinaigrette in a screw-top jar and shake vigorously to combine thoroughly.

Arrange the stuffed cabbage on a serving dish, mixing the coloured leaves together. Pour over the vinaigrette. Allow to stand for a few minutes before serving.

TIME: *Preparation takes about 15 minutes, plus standing.*
Cooking takes approximately 1 hour.

Minty Cucumber Pieces

MAKES APPROXIMATELY 24 PIECES

Both mint and cucumber have a very clean taste so they work well together

INGREDIENTS

1 large cucumber

lots of fresh mint leaves

12g/½oz sugar

50ml/2fl oz olive oil

50ml/2fl oz white wine vinegar

salt and freshly ground black pepper

125g/4oz soft cream cheese

52

▌ Using a potato peeler, remove strips of skin from the full length of the cucumber so you are left with an alternating pattern of peeled and unpeeled.

▌ Cut the cucumber in half lengthways and, using a teaspoon, carefully remove the seeds from the centre of both halves. Cut each half into roughly 2.5cm/1-inch chunks and place in a bowl.

▌ Take a good handful of fresh mint leaves, rinse under cold running water and drain thoroughly. Sprinkle over the sugar over and chop very finely.

▌ Place the chopped mint in a screw-topped jar along with the olive oil, white wine vinegar and seasoning. Shake well to mix the ingredients.

▌ Pour the marinade over the prepared cucumber, cover and refrigerate for a couple of hours.

▌ Wash and finely chop another handful of mint leaves and beat into the cream cheese along with a little seasoning.

▌ Remove the cucumber from the bowl and drain off any surplus marinade. Spoon the minty cream cheese into a piping bag with a decorative nozzle and pipe a line of cheese in the centre of each piece of cucumber.

▌ Arrange the cucumber on a serving dish and refrigerate until required.

TIME: *Preparation takes about 30 minutes, plus marinating.*

Aunt Ada's Potatoes

SERVES 4

This dish serves 4 as a vegetable accompaniment or 2 as a main course

INGREDIENTS
2 large baking potatoes, evenly sized

a little oil

2 egg yolks

125g/4oz Red Leicester cheese, grated

salt and freshly ground black pepper

25g/1oz salted peanuts

60ml/4tbsp fresh breadcrumbs

25g/1oz grated Parmesan cheese

a little melted butter

Scrub the potatoes under cold running water and prick all over with a fork. Brush the potatoes with a little oil if desired, this will give them a shiny finish. Place the potatoes directly onto the shelf of a preheated oven at 220°C/425°F/Gas Mark 7 for approximately an hour or until the potato feels soft inside when gently squeezed.

Take a sharp knife and cut the baked potatoes in half. Scoop out the flesh into a mixing bowl, leaving a thin layer next to the skin.

Mash the potato and beat in the egg yolks one at a time, then stir in the Red Leicester cheese and season well.

Using the back of a knife lightly crush the peanuts and mix them with the breadcrumbs and grated Parmesan cheese. Pile the potato mixture back into the skins and sprinkle generously with the breadcrumb mixture.

Drizzle a little melted butter over the tops of the potatoes and return them to the oven for 15 minutes until they have heated through. Place under a preheated grill for a few minutes prior to serving.

TIME: *Preparation takes about 20 minutes. Cooking takes approximately 1 hour 15 minutes.*

54

Cheese-stuffed Battered Mushrooms with Blueberry Sauce

SERVES 4

These mushrooms would be great as a starter or as part of a finger buffet

INGREDIENTS

12 medium cup mushrooms

225g/8oz cream cheese

4 spring onions, finely chopped

oil for deep frying

FOR THE BATTER

125g/4oz plain flour

pinch of salt

15ml/1tbsp olive oil

150ml/5fl oz water

1 egg white

FOR THE SAUCE

225g/8oz fresh blueberries

50g/2oz caster sugar

a little water

Make the batter first as fritter batter benefits greatly from standing for a while. Sift the flour and salt into a mixing bowl and make a well in the centre. Pour in the olive oil and water and beat with a wooden spoon, gradually incorporating all the flour until you have a thick, smooth batter. Cover and leave for an hour. Just prior to using, stiffly beat the egg white and fold it in.

To make the blueberry sauce, put all the ingredients in a saucepan and place over a low heat, stirring regularly, until the fruit has softened and the sauce has thickened and reduced a little. Keep warm until serving.

Carefully remove the stalks from the mushrooms and discard. Beat the cream cheese in a bowl until it becomes soft then add the spring onions and continue beating for a minute or two.

Taking teaspoonfuls of the cream cheese mixture, stuff the mushroom caps generously and smooth over the surface.

Heat the oil for deep frying in a large saucepan. It has reached the correct temperature when traces of blue smoke begin to rise from the oil. Dip the mushrooms into the batter one at a time and let any excess batter run back into the bowl. Fry no more than 2 mushrooms at a time so you can keep an eye on their progress, they will take approximately 2–3 minutes to cook to a lovely golden brown.

Keep the cooked mushrooms hot until they are all fried, then serve accompanied by a sauceboat of blueberry sauce.

TIME: *Preparation takes about 20 minutes. Cooking takes approximately 25 minutes.*

Individual Tomato Salads

SERVES *4*

A *slice of Italian sunshine*

INGREDIENTS

4 ripe beef tomatoes

225g/8oz mozzarella cheese, cubed

225g/8oz black olives, pitted

1 red onion, thinly sliced

15ml/1tbsp chopped oregano leaves

olive oil and black pepper, to serve

FOR THE DRESSING

50ml/2fl oz olive oil

25ml/1fl oz white wine vinegar

salt and freshly ground black pepper

❚ Cut the tops from the tomatoes and using a teaspoon, remove the insides and discard.

❚ Place the next 4 ingredients in a bowl and lightly mix.

❚ Put the dressing ingredients in a screw-top jar and shake thoroughly to mix. Pour over the filling, mix with the fingertips and season generously.

❚ Spoon the filling into the tomato shells and spoon over any remaining dressing. Replace the lids.

❚ Arrange the tomatoes on a serving dish, brush the outsides with a little olive oil and grind over lots of black pepper so that it sticks to the shells.

TIME: *Preparation takes about 30 minutes.*

Stuffed Baby Bell Peppers

SERVES *4*

T*hese sweet-tasting peppers are a joy to cook with*

INGREDIENTS

8 red baby bell peppers

225g/8oz tub plain cottage cheese

30ml/2tbsp snipped chives

salt and freshly ground black pepper

few frisée lettuce leaves, washed

45ml/3tbsp olive oil

12 pitted black olives, cut into rings

juice of 1 lemon

❚ Remove stalks from the peppers and cut them in half lengthways. Carefully pull out the core and seeds and set the peppers to one side briefly.

❚ Empty the cottage cheese into a mixing bowl and stir in the snipped chives and plenty of black pepper. Using a teaspoon fill the peppers with the cottage cheese mixture and arrange them on a serving platter lined with the washed lettuce leaves.

❚ Place the olive oil, lemon juice and plenty of seasoning in a screw-top jar and shake vigorously to mix.

❚ Pour the dressing over the stuffed peppers and scatter with the sliced olives. Keep refrigerated until required.

TIME: *Preparation takes about 30 minutes.*

Cheese Soufflé Potatoes

SERVES 4

Soufflés are not difficult to prepare and look very impressive when served

INGREDIENTS

4 large baking potatoes

25g/1oz butter

25g/1oz plain flour

300ml/10fl oz milk

salt and freshly ground black pepper

2 eggs, separated

125g/4oz freshly grated Parmesan

freshly grated nutmeg

Scrub the potatoes under cold running water and prick all over with a fork.

Place the potatoes directly onto the shelf of a preheated oven at 220°C/425°F/Gas Mark 7 for about an hour or until the potato feels soft when gently squeezed. When the potatoes are cooked reduce the oven temperature to 200°C/400°F/Gas Mark 6.

Melt the butter in a saucepan over a low heat and add the flour, stir the two together for a few minutes to allow the flour to cook. Slowly add the milk a little at a time to begin with then increase the flow, stirring all the time, until all the milk has been incorporated and the sauce is thick and smooth.

Cut a slice from the top of each potato and scoop out the soft potato flesh, leaving a thick wall against the skin. Mash the potato well and beat in the egg yolks and plenty of seasoning.

Add the thick sauce and grated Parmesan and continue beating until they are well combined. In a separate bowl whisk the egg whites until stiff and, using a metal spoon, carefully fold them into the sauce.

Spoon the soufflé mixture back into the potato shells and grate a little fresh nutmeg into each potato. Return the potatoes to the oven and continue cooking for a further 20 minutes until the soufflé is risen and browned. Serve immediately.

TIME: *Preparation takes about 35 minutes. Cooking takes approximately 1 hour 20 minutes.*

58

Baked Potatoes with Cauliflower & Almond Curry

SERVES 4

This spicy vegetarian curry goes very well with baked potatoes

INGREDIENTS

4 large baking potatoes, evenly sized

50g/2oz butter

1 onion, thinly sliced

1tsp ground turmeric

2tsp ground coriander

1tsp ground cumin

1 small cauliflower

50g/2oz blanched almonds, roughly chopped

50g/2oz frozen peas, defrosted

50g/2oz desiccated coconut

mango chutney, to serve

❚ Scrub the potatoes under cold running water and prick with a fork.

❚ Place directly onto the shelf of a preheated oven at 220°C/425°F/Gas Mark 7 for about an hour or until the potatoes feel soft when gently squeezed.

❚ While they are cooking prepare the curry. Melt the butter in a frying pan and fry the sliced onion until soft and golden brown.

❚ Add the spices to the pan and fry, stirring continuously for a few minutes.

❚ Cut the cauliflower into small florets and add to the pan along with the almonds and peas. Gently stir the vegetables so they become coated in spice then add sufficient cold water to moisten the curry and create a small amount of sauce.

❚ Gently simmer the curry for about 10 minutes, adding a little extra water as and when necessary.

❚ When all the vegetables are tender sprinkle over the coconut and stir it into the curry. Continue cooking for a few minutes longer then remove the pan from the heat.

❚ When the potatoes have finished baking, split them in half and scoop out some of the cooked insides. Roughly chop half of the potato flesh and add it to the curry.

❚ Reheat the curry briefly and share it between the potatoes. Serve immediately accompanied by mango chutney.

TIME: *Preparation takes about 20 minutes. Cooking takes approximately 1 hour.*

59

Globe Artichoke with Hollandaise Sauce

SERVES 4

The globe artichoke is a tasty but often overlooked vegetable

INGREDIENTS

4 medium globe artichokes

10ml/2tsp lemon juice

salt and freshly ground black pepper

3 egg yolks

225g/8oz cold butter

fresh nutmeg

Cut the stalk off the artichokes as close to the base of the vegetable as possible. Remove any discoloured outer leaves as they are likely to be tough, and snip off the tips of the remaining leaves with a sharp pair of scissors.

Add a few drops of lemon juice to a saucepan of salted water, bring to the boil and drop in the prepared artichokes. Cover and leave to simmer gently for approximately 40 minutes.

The sauce is very simple to make but must not be hurried or the eggs will cook too much and scramble. Place the egg yolks and 10ml/2tsp lemon juice in a heat-resistant bowl, season well and stand over a saucepan of gently bubbling water.

Using a balloon whisk, whisk the mixture for a few minutes until it thickens a little. Remove the butter from the fridge and chop it into pieces not much bigger than a pea. Feed these slowly into the egg yolks, one at a time, making sure that each is incorporated into the sauce before another is added.

Slowly the sauce will thicken and when complete will have the look and consistency of fresh mayonnaise. As the sauce never gets hot during cooking, it should be kept at similarly low temperatures until served. This is best achieved by standing the bowl of sauce in warm water.

When the artichokes are tender, remove them from the water and drain briefly upside down on absorbent kitchen paper. When well drained use a teaspoon to gently scrape away and remove the choke from the centre of the vegetable.

Place the artichokes on a serving dish and spoon the Hollandaise sauce into the centre of each. Grate over a little fresh nutmeg and serve immediately.

TIME: *Preparation takes about 30 minutes. Cooking takes approximately 45 minutes.*

61

Mushrooms with Pine Nuts & Tapenade

SERVES 4

A *simple starter or snack full of Mediterranean flavours*

INGREDIENTS

8 large flat cap mushrooms

60ml/4tbsp tapenade (olive paste)

30ml/2tbsp pine nuts

30ml/2tbsp fresh breadcrumbs

salt and freshly ground black pepper

olive oil

❙ Wipe the mushroom caps and cut off as much of the stalk as possible. Place gills upwards on a lightly oiled baking sheet.

❙ Divide the tapenade between the mushrooms and gently spread it out to completely cover the gills.

❙ Crush the pine nuts using a pestle and mortar or the heel of a knife and sprinkle them over the tapenade. Top with a layer of breadcrumbs and a little seasoning.

❙ Drizzle a little olive oil over the mushrooms and place under a preheated grill for 5–10 minutes until the top of the stuffing has browned and the mushrooms are tender.

TIME: *Preparation takes about 15 minutes. Cooking takes approximately 10 minutes.*

Rice-stuffed Peppers

SERVES 4

T*he pesto livens up the rice filling*

INGREDIENTS

4 squat green peppers

olive oil

salt and freshly ground black pepper

FOR THE FILLING

350g/12oz cooked long grain and wild rice mixture

50g/2oz roughly chopped walnuts

15ml/1tbsp flaked almonds, toasted

30ml/2tbsp green pesto

125g/4oz dried prunes, stoned and chopped

❙ Cut the tops from the peppers and remove the seeds and core. Place the peppers and lids in a large bowl and pour over sufficient boiling water to cover them. Allow to stand for 5 minutes then pour off the water and drain the pepper shells upside-down on kitchen paper.

❙ Mix together all the filling ingredients. Season well and pack into the pepper shells.

❙ Place on a baking sheet, cover with the pepper tops and lightly brush with a little olive oil. Grind over some black pepper and place them in a preheated oven at 180°C/350°F/Gas Mark 4 for 40 minutes.

TIME: *Preparation takes about 20 minutes. Cooking takes approximately 1 hour.*

62

Stir-fried Vegetables on Aubergine Rafts

SERVES 4

Stir-frying baby vegetables keeps all the fresh flavours intact

INGREDIENTS

2 medium aubergines

salt

60ml/4tbsp olive oil

30ml/2tbsp peanut oil

1 bunch spring onions, sliced diagonally

450g/16oz mixed baby vegetables such as

sweetcorn, carrots, French beans, button mushrooms

50g/2oz unsalted peanuts

30ml/2tbsp sesame seeds

15ml/1tbsp light soy sauce

▌Cut each aubergine lengthways into 4 thick slices, lay on a baking sheet and sprinkle liberally with salt.

▌Leave the aubergines for 30 minutes to extract the bitter juices then rinse off under cold running water and pat dry.

▌Reserve the 2 inner slices from each aubergine for frying, 2 outer slices should be chopped to roughly the same size as the baby vegetables.

▌Heat 30ml/2tbsp of the olive oil in a frying pan and fry 2 of the aubergine slices until tender and lightly browned. Place them in a moderate oven to keep hot while you repeat the process with the remaining olive oil and the other 2 slices. Keep hot while you stir-fry the vegetables.

▌Heat the peanut oil in a wok or high-sided frying pan and fry the spring onions for approximately 3 minutes.

▌Add the baby vegetables and chopped aubergine to the pan and continue cooking for a further 3 minutes until they are cooked but still crisp.

▌Add the peanuts and sesame seeds and fry for another minute then add the soy sauce and heat through briefly.

▌Remove the fried aubergine slices from the oven, transfer them to their serving dishes and spoon the stir-fried vegetables over the top. Serve immediately.

TIME: *Preparation takes about 10 minutes. Cooking takes approximately 20 minutes.*

Multicoloured Roast Peppers with Ratatouille

SERVES 6

It *is hard to imagine a more colourful dish*

INGREDIENTS

1 large aubergine, thickly sliced

salt and freshly ground black pepper

6 large peppers, as many different colours as possible

olive oil

2 medium onions, thinly sliced

4 cloves garlic, roughly chopped

4 courgettes, thinly sliced

10ml/2tsp dried thyme

stalk of fresh rosemary

2x400g/14oz cans chopped tomatoes

15ml/1tbsp tomato purée

fresh chopped parsley (for garnish)

freshly grated Parmesan cheese

Spread the aubergine slices over a baking sheet and sprinkle generously with salt, set aside for 30 minutes to extract the bitter juices.

Cut all the peppers in half lengthways through the stalk and remove the core and seeds.

Arrange the peppers on a baking sheet, brush with a little olive oil and grind over plenty of black pepper. Set aside briefly.

Heat 60ml/4tbsp olive oil in a large saucepan and fry the sliced onion and garlic until soft and golden brown. Rinse off the aubergine slices and add to the pan along with the courgettes. Fry for a couple of minutes so they can absorb the garlic-flavoured oil.

Add the dried thyme and fresh rosemary and fry for a few seconds before adding the canned tomatoes and tomato purée.

Season well and leave to simmer, uncovered, over a low heat until the sauce thickens and the vegetables are cooked but retain their shape.

While the ratatouille is cooking place the tray of peppers into a preheated oven at 180°C/350°F/Gas Mark 4 and cook until they soften and the skins catch slightly. Cooking peppers this way intensifies the already bright colours of the flesh and they look stunning.

This dish looks most impressive brought to the table on a large round or oval serving plate. Carefully arrange the roasted peppers around the edge of the dish in alternating colours with the stalks facing outwards.

Fish out the rosemary stalk and ladle spoonfuls of the ratatouille over the peppers, leaving the stalk end exposed.

Grate over lots of black pepper and scatter over handfuls of roughly chopped parsley.

Serve straightaway with a bowl of freshly grated Parmesan cheese for sprinkling.

TIME: *Preparation takes about 30 minutes, plus standing.*
Cooking takes approximately 45 minutes.

*M*ushrooms on *M*ushrooms

S E R V E S   4

*F*or real mushroom addicts!

INGREDIENTS

50g/2oz dried Ceps

8 large flat mushrooms

30ml/2tbsp olive oil

50g/2oz Oyster mushrooms

125g/4oz Shiitake mushrooms

3 cloves garlic, chopped

15ml/1tbsp pine nuts

60ml/4tbsp grated Parmesan cheese

freshly ground black pepper

chopped parsley, to garnish

▍Place the dried Ceps in a small amount of tepid water for 20 minutes to reconstitute.

▍Wipe the caps of the large flat mushrooms and cut off the stalk. Place gills upwards on a baking sheet brushed with a little olive oil.

▍When the Ceps are ready, drain the water from them and roughly chop them with the Oyster and Shiitake mushrooms.

▍Heat the olive oil in a frying pan and fry the chopped garlic until brown.

▍Add the chopped mushrooms to the pan and fry, tossing them in the oil until they have absorbed the oil and garlic flavour. Add the pine nuts to the pan and stir to coat them in the oil.

▍Spoon the topping onto the large mushroom caps and pour over any surplus cooking liquor. Cover loosely with foil and place in a preheated oven at 180°C/350°F/Gas Mark 4 for 15 minutes until the large mushrooms are just tender.

▍Remove the foil and share the grated Parmesan between the mushrooms. Grind some black pepper over each one and place under a preheated grill until the cheese melts and turns golden brown.

▍Generously garnish with chopped parsley and transfer to serving dishes. Serve with plenty of fresh bread to soak up the juices.

TIME: *Preparation takes about 10 minutes, plus soaking.*

Cooking takes approximately 30 minutes.

Blue Vinney Parsnip Peppers

SERVES 4

This recipe brings a new dimension to stuffed peppers

INGREDIENTS

225g/8oz parsnips

4 squat yellow peppers, evenly sized

50g/2oz butter

50g/2oz plain flour

300ml/10fl oz fresh milk

175g/6oz Blue Vinney cheese (or Blue Stilton)

50g/2oz walnut pieces

25g/1oz sultanas

salt and freshly ground black pepper

20ml/4tsp green pesto

Peel the parsnips and cut them into even-sized pieces of roughly 2cm/³/4-inch square. Blanch in boiling water for about 5 minutes then drain and set aside on absorbent kitchen paper until required.

Cut the tops from the peppers, remove the seeds and place in a large bowl with their tops. Pour over sufficient boiling water to cover, leave to stand for about 5 minutes then drain off the water.

Melt the butter in a saucepan over a low heat, add the flour and stir for a couple of minutes to allow the flour to cook. Gradually add the milk to the pan, stirring all the time, until you have a thick, smooth sauce.

Remove the rind from the cheese and discard. Chop the cheese into small pieces and stir into the sauce along with the walnut pieces, sultanas and blanched parsnip. Gently stir the sauce to combine the ingredients and finish with plenty of seasoning.

Spread a teaspoon of pesto over the inside of each pepper and fill to the brim with spoonfuls of the cheese and parsnip sauce. Push out the green stalk from the tops of the peppers and place one on top of each pepper to make a lid.

Place in a preheated oven at 170°C/ 325°F/Gas Mark 3 for 35–40 minutes until the flesh of the peppers is tender and the tops are just beginning to brown. Serve immediately.

TIME: *Preparation takes about 15 minutes. Cooking takes approximately 1 hour.*

Aubergine Provençale

SERVES 4

This is an all-in-one vegetable dish

INGREDIENTS

2 large aubergines

90ml/6tbsp olive oil

1 large onion, thinly sliced

2 cloves garlic, roughly chopped

1 red pepper, seeded and chopped

2 courgettes, thinly sliced

stalk of fresh rosemary

1 bay leaf

400g/14oz can chopped tomatoes

150ml/5fl oz red wine

salt and freshly ground black pepper

60ml/4tbsp Parmesan cheese, grated

❚ Cut the aubergines in half lengthways and sprinkle the cut surface with salt. Allow to stand for 30 minutes to extract the bitter juices then rinse off the salt and pat dry.

❚ While the aubergine is standing, begin preparing the filling. Heat 60ml/4tbsp of olive oil in a large saucepan and fry the onion and garlic until lightly browned.

❚ Add the pepper and courgettes to the pan and continue frying for a couple of minutes until they begin to soften.

❚ Drop the stalk of rosemary and the bay leaf into the pan. Stir into the vegetables briefly then add the chopped tomatoes and red wine. Season well and leave on a low heat to simmer gently for about 20 minutes.

❚ Heat the remaining olive oil in a frying pan and fry the aubergine halves for a couple of minutes on each side. Lift out of the pan when cooked and drain them on absorbent kitchen paper. Set aside to cool.

❚ Scoop out the cooled aubergine flesh with a spoon, leaving a thin layer next to the skin. Roughly chop the aubergine and add it to the vegetables.

❚ The filling is ready when the vegetables are cooked but still retain their shape and the sauce is thick and glossy. Remove the rosemary and bay leaf and correct the seasoning.

❚ Arrange the aubergine 'shells' on a baking sheet and spoon generous quantities of filling into each one. Sprinkle with grated Parmesan.

❚ Place in a preheated oven at 200°C/400°F/Gas Mark 6 for 10 minutes to heat through thoroughly and melt the cheese into a crust.

TIME: *Preparation takes about 30 minutes, plus standing.*
Cooking takes approximately 50 minutes.

Oh So Garlicky Peppers

SERVES 4

This recipe is one for real lovers of garlic

INGREDIENTS

8 baby bell peppers

8 cloves garlic, peeled

salt and freshly ground black pepper

olive oil

4 shallots, very finely chopped

1 red chilli, seeded and chopped

125g/4oz pitted black olives, finely chopped

fresh breadcrumbs

Cut the tops from the peppers and carefully remove the seeds and core. Rub the inside of each pepper with a clove of garlic and set to one side.

To make the garlic into a paste suitable for frying, place the cloves on a non-absorbent work surface and sprinkle with a little salt. Begin chopping them with the heel of a large knife. As the garlic is chopped the salt will draw the moisture from inside the cloves and you will soon have a useable paste.

Heat 30ml/2tbsp of olive oil in a small frying pan and fry the shallots and chopped chilli until they are soft. Try not to let the shallots brown. Add the garlic paste and continue frying for a minute, then add the chopped olives and fry for a further minute.

Season well, then begin adding breadcrumbs a tablespoon at a time, stirring continually, until you have sufficient stuffing for the peppers.

Remove the pan from the heat and using a teaspoon, pack the garlic stuffing into the baby peppers. Place the lids on top and lightly brush the outsides of the peppers with a little olive oil, grind some black pepper over and arrange the peppers on a baking sheet.

Place in a preheated oven at 180°C/350°F/Gas Mark 4 and cook for approximately 15–20 minutes or until the flesh is tender.

When cooked, transfer the peppers to a serving dish and serve either as a starter or as a vegetable accompaniment to a main course.

TIME: *Preparation takes about 25 minutes.*
Cooking takes approximately 40 minutes.

Plum Tomatoes with Horseradish & Watercress Pasta

SERVES 4

Sweet-tasting plum tomatoes contrast sharply with this mayonnaise

INGREDIENTS

salt and freshly ground black pepper

225g/8oz small pasta (e.g. conchiglie or piccole)

olive oil

4 large plum tomatoes, slightly under-ripe

45ml/3tbsp fresh mayonnaise (see page 11)

10ml/2tsp cream of horseradish sauce

25g/1oz raisins

1 bunch watercress

▌Bring a saucepan of lightly salted water to the boil and drop in the pasta with a little olive oil to prevent sticking. Cook the pasta until just tender *(al dente)*, then drain off the cooking water.

▌Toss the cooked pasta in a sprinkling of olive oil and set aside to cool.

▌Cut the plum tomatoes in half lengthways and using a teaspoon scoop out the insides and discard, taking care not to damage the skins. Set aside.

▌Place the mayonnaise in a bowl and beat in the horseradish sauce and raisins. Season well.

▌Discard any rough-looking watercress and wash the remainder in plenty of cold water. Drain and shake thoroughly to remove as much water as possible then cut off most of the stalks. Finely chop the remaining watercress to a fine pulp and stir into the mayonnaise.

▌Stir the mayonnaise into the cooled pasta adding a small amount at a time. Add just enough to bind the pasta together and create a little surplus sauce. If there is any mayonnaise left over it is better to refrigerate it for future use than use too much.

▌Spoon generous quantities of the pasta salad into the tomato shells and transfer them to serving dishes. Serve with brown bread and butter and the pepper mill.

TIME: *Preparation takes about 30 minutes. Cooking takes approximately 5 minutes.*

Leeky Potatoes

SERVES 4

Lightly fried leeks and a good cheese sauce were made for each other

INGREDIENTS

4 large baking potatoes

2 medium leeks

25g/1oz butter

25g/1oz flour

300ml/10fl oz fresh milk

30ml/2tbsp olive oil

125g/4oz strong cheddar cheese, grated

1 egg yolk

salt and freshly ground black pepper

▌Scrub the potatoes under cold running water and prick all over with a fork. Place directly onto the shelf of a preheated oven at 220°C/425°F/Gas Mark 7 for approximately 1 hour or until the potato feels soft when gently squeezed. .

▌While the potatoes are baking prepare the filling. Make a deep cut into each leek roughly three-quarters of its length and wash the insides thoroughly to remove any soil. Set to one side to drain.

▌To make the cheese sauce, melt the butter over a low heat, add the flour and stir the two together for a couple of minutes to allow the flour to cook.

▌Slowly add the milk a little at a time to begin with, stirring continuously, then increase the flow until all the milk is used and you have a thick, smooth sauce.

▌Stir in 50g/2oz of the grated Cheddar cheese and plenty of seasoning. Set the sauce to one side.

▌Cut the cleaned leeks in half and slice each one into 2cm/3/4-inch lengths.

▌Heat the olive oil in a frying pan and fry the leeks for a couple of minutes until they are softened but not browned. Stir the cooked leeks into the cheese sauce.

▌When the potatoes are cooked, slice a lid from the top of each one and scoop out the soft flesh using a teaspoon, leaving a good layer of potato next to the skin.

▌Mash half of the potato innards with the egg yolk, the remaining grated cheese and freshly ground black pepper, and share equally between the potato shells.

▌Fill the potatoes to the top with the cheese and leek mixture and cover with the lids. Return to the oven for 10 minutes to heat through and serve immediately.

TIME: *Preparation takes about 25 minutes. Cooking takes approximately 1 hour 10 minutes.*

Onion & Goats' Cheese

SERVES 4

Goats' cheese is the essence of France

INGREDIENTS

2 medium red onions

olive oil

350g/12oz goats' cheese

50g/2oz pine nuts

handful of fresh basil leaves

▌ Place the unpeeled onions onto the shelf of a preheated oven at 200°C/400°F/Gas Mark 6 for 20 minutes.

▌ Carefully remove the skin from the part-cooked onions and cut them in half through the root end. Remove a few of the inner layers of onion to create an onion bowl, brush with a little olive oil and place on a baking sheet.

▌ Chop the goats' cheese into small pieces and place in a bowl with the pine nuts. Bruise the basil with the handle of a knife to release the flavour, then tear into the bowl.

▌ Brush a little olive oil onto the fingertips and lightly mix the stuffing ingredients together. Place handfuls of the mixture in the onion bowls. Do not overfill the onions. Store any leftover stuffing in the fridge.

▌ Reduce the oven temperature to 180°C/350°F/Gas Mark 4 and return the stuffed onions to the oven for 10–15 minutes or until the cheese has softened.

▌ Serve with plenty of cheese biscuits and French bread and perhaps a glass or two of port.

TIME: *Preparation takes about 25 minutes. Cooking takes approximately 35 minutes.*

Artichoke Hearts with Tapenade

SERVES 4

The Italian artichoke and the French tapenade combine beautifully

INGREDIENTS

2 cans large artichoke hearts

60ml/4tbsp tapenade (olive paste)

2 egg yolks, lightly beaten

fresh breadcrumbs for coating

salt and freshly ground black pepper

oil for deep frying

tomato sauce for dipping

▌ Remove artichokes from the cans and drain thoroughly. If possible choose larger artichokes for this recipe as they are easier to prepare and look better when served.

▌ Cut the hearts in half from top to bottom and carefully remove one or two of the layers from the middle of each half. Spoon a little tapenade into each cavity.

▌ Dip the stuffed artichokes into the beaten egg yolk and roll in breadcrumbs seasoned with a little salt and pepper.

▌ Heat the oil in a deep-fat fryer and cook 2 or 3 at a time until golden.

▌ Lift the cooked artichokes from the oil on a slotted spoon and transfer to absorbent kitchen paper.

▌ When they are all cooked transfer them to a suitable dish and serve immediately with tomato sauce.

TIME: *Preparation takes about 20 minutes. Cooking takes approximately 15 minutes.*

Index